Good Neighbors and Other Moral
Stories

Adapted from Arabic by
Assad Nimer Busool
Ph.D. Islamic & Arabic Studies

Copyright 1993 by
IQRA' International Educational Foundation   Chicago

**Part of a Comprehensive
and Systematic Program
of Islamic Studies**

**Program of
Qur'anic Studies**

Chief Program Editors:

Abidullah al-Ansari Ghazi
Ph.D. History of Religion, Harvard

Tasneema Khatoon Ghazi
Ph.D. Curriculum and Reading,
University of Minnesota

Approved by:

Rabita al-Alam al-Islami
Makkah Mukarramah

Reviewers:

Noura Durkee

Fadel Abdullah

Language Editors:

Hena Azam

Designed By

George Gabriel

Good Neighbors

For my son,
Nimer

A NOTE TO READERS

It is part of Islamic Akhlaq (etiquette) to show respect for Rasulullah by saying:

Salla-Allahu-`alaihi-wa-sallam

(May peace and blessings be upon him)
whenever we take his name. In this book,
we have abbreviated this as (S) to remind the reader to say it in his mind whenever he sees his name.

Similarly, we show respect for the Sahabah of Rasulullah by saying:

Radiy-Allahu ta'ala `anhu

(May Allah be pleased with him)
In this book, we have abbreviated this as (R) as a reminder to the reader to invoke Allah's blessings.

Whenever we take Allah's name, we must praise and glorify Him by saying:

Subhanahu-wa-ta'ala

(May He be Exalted, Glorified)
So, whenever His name is used, (SWT) follows as a reminder.

Islamic Morals
Theory and Practice

I. Definition of moral.
    The New Century Dictionary of the English
    Language.
    Moral: Pertaining to or concerned with right
    conduct, or the distinction between
    right and wrong...; concerned with the
    principles of rules of right conduct
    ethical; also, expressing or conveying truths
    or counsel as to right conduct..., also,
    conforming to the rules of right conduct...

II. The Islamic code of moral behavior is set
    down in detail in the Qur'an. It covers
    social interaction, business, government, Social
    relations with others (Muslims, Jews,
    Christians and non-believers.)

    Allah said in the Qur'an:
    O you who believe! Stand out firmly for justice,
    as witnesses to Allah, even against yourselves,
    or your parents, or your kin, and whether he is
    rich or poor: For Allah can best protect you
    distort [justice] or decline to do justice, verily
    Allah is well-acquainted with all that you do.
    (al-Nissa' 4/135)

III. Moral behavior was exemplified by the Prophet (S) in his daily life so that his followers could follow his Sunnah.

Before his death, the Prophet (S) told his followers:
"I am leaving for you the Book of God (*The Qur'an*) and the Sunnah of His Prophet, if you follow them you will never go astray."

IV. This moral code must be followed by all Muslims, irrespective to their position and status.

V. Throughout the ages, morality has been the subject of literature in the Muslim World.

Ahmad Shawqi, a modern Arab poet (d. 1932), wrote as thus of the morality of people:

Indeed, the morals are the people. All the time the morals exist, the people exist.
However, if the morals cease to exist, The people will perish.

The following anecdotes were selected from variety of classic literary and historical Arabic sources

Criticizing Others' Faults

Hatim once advised someone:
> "If you see a fault of your friend, and you
> keep it from him, you betray him; and
> if you face him with it, you alienate him."

The man asked him:
> "In such situation, what should be done?"

Hatim replied:
> "Speak indirectly hinting at it, and making
> it as a part of general conversation.
> After all, it is the correction of the fault
> you require, not the disgrace of someone."

Forgiveness

'Umar Ibn 'Abd al-'Aziz ordered punishment
for a man in his absence. He vowed to
punish him severely, if Allah (SWT) helped
him capture the man. 'Umar succeeded
in capturing the man, and he proceeded to
punish him. Raja' Ibn Haywah, his
minister, said to him:

> "Allah (SWT) already did for you what you
> wished the most. Now you do what
> Allah (SWT) likes the most — forgive."

Hearing this, 'Umar forgave the man and
allowed him to go free.

Man's Enemy

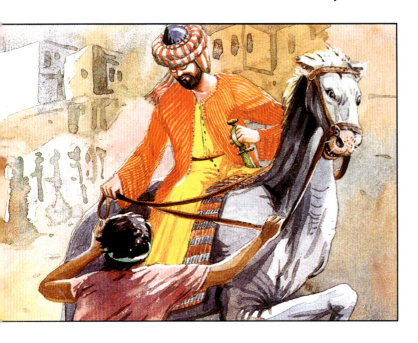

Once, while 'Abd Allah Ibn Ja'far was riding his
horse, a man suddenly blocked his way.
Grabbing 'Abd Allah's horse he said:

"O Prince, cut my neck for Allah's sake."

Hearing this, 'Abd Allah stared at him
and said:

"Are you crazy?"

The man replied:

"By Allah, I am not crazy, but I am in
a condition which is worse than death."

'Abd-Allah then asked:

"Tell me, what is the matter?"

The man explained:

"I have a bitter enemy, who is persistently,
tightening his grip on me, and I have

no power to escape."

'Abd Allah asked:

"Who is this enemy, whose oppression is
making you prefer death over life?"

The man answered:

"Poverty is my enemy."

Hearing this, 'Abd Allah instructed his servant:

"Give him a thousand dinars."

Then he turned to the man and said:

"My dear brother, take it, but if
your enemy comes back to harass you,
come to me and I will do justice,
Insha' Allah."

The man said:

"By Allah, I have received enough
of your generosity to help me defeat my
enemy for the rest of my life."

Contented Beggar

Once, the money changers in Egypt met in a
Masjid to weigh the dinars and the gold for
the Sultan. Meanwhile, a poor man came from
one of the corners of the Masjid and asked
them for half a dirham of silver, but they did
not give it to him. However, when they left, they
forgot a bag containing five hundred dinars.
The poor man found it, took it and buried it in
the floor of the Masjid. Soon after this, the
money changers came back and asked:

> "O poor man, we forgot a bag of five
> hundred dinars here."

The poor man unearthed the bag and handed

it to them. They then opened the bag and gave the poor man fifty dinars, as a reward for his honesty. The poor man said:

"I do not want them."

They said to him:

"You asked for a half a dirham from us, and now you are refusing fifty dinars?"

The poor man explained:

"I asked for something because of my need, but I do not want a reward for my honesty. I don't want to sell the big reward of the Hereafter for a small reward in this world."

Worth of a Kingdom

Al-Khalifah Harun al-Rashid asked Ibn
al-Sammak, who was known for his wisdom and
piety, for advice. Al-Rashid had a glass
of water in his hand at that moment. Ibn
al-Sammak said:

> "O Amir al-Mu'minin[1], if you were thirsty
> and were forbidden to have this
> drink of water, would you exchange it for
> your kingdom?"

Al-Rashid answered:

> "Yes."

Ibn al-Sammak then asked:

> "If you drank it, and it could not be
> expelled, and you were in severe pain,

1 Commander of the
faithful, a title for the
Caliph (*Khalifah*)

would you exchange this pain for your kingdom?"

Al-Rashid responded:

"Of course, to be freed of the pain, I would."

Ibn al-Sammak remarked:

"Then there is no good in a kingdom which is not even worth a drink of water."

The Burden of Debt

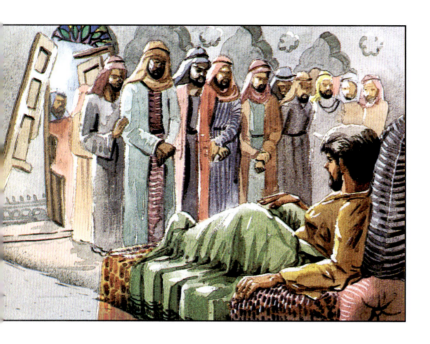

Qays Ibn Sa‘d Ibn ‘Ubadah was rich and
generous, always eager to help people in need.
Once he got sick, but none of his friends
came to visit him. He was surprised by this lack
of concern from his friends and asked for
the reason. He was told:

> "People feel uneasy to come and visit you
> because of their indebtedness to you."

He said:

> "May Allah (SWT) cast shame on
> the wealth which prevents friends from
> visiting their friends."

Then he made a public announcement:
> "Whoever owes Qays any debt, is released
> from it."

That evening, the threshold of his door was
broken because of the large number
of visitors who came to see him and thank him.

Gift or Bribe?

'Umar Ibn 'Abd al-'Aziz once expressed
a desire to have Lebanese apples. A basket
of Lebanese apples was brought to him,
but he did not accept it. It was said to him:
> "You know that the Prophet (S) used
> to accept gifts."

'Umar replied:
> "The gift for the Prophet (S)
> was indeed a gift, but for a government
> official, it is a bribe."

Ranking People

Bakr Ibn 'Abd Allah advised his brother:
> "Rank people into three categories in relation to you."

His brother asked:
> "How should I rank them?"

Bakr replied:
> "Treat those who are older than you as you would your father, those who are of your age as your brothers, and those who are younger than you as your sons. Then see which one of those you would ever expose or scandalize."

Piety

One who makes   1
the *adhan*, the call for
prayer

Al-Khalifah Sulaiman Ibn 'Abd al-Malik had a
Mu'adhdhin[1] who called *Adhan* for prayers
in the Masjid of the palace. One of Sulaiman's
favorite maids told him that the *Mu'adhdhin*
keep staring at her whenever she passed by
him. The report by the maid greatly
annoyed Sulaiman, a very jealous man. He
asked her:

> "Beautify yourself and wear perfume, and
> go back to the *Mu'adhdhin* and tell him,
> 'I notice your interest in me, and I
> feel for you more than you feel for me. I
> came to you out of my love for you
> and *Amir al-Mu'minin* is not aware of this.'"

So she went to the *Mu'adhdhin* and told him

what she had been ordered to. The *Mu'adhdhin* raised his eyes up toward the sky and said:

"O God! I fear you."

Then he told the maid,

"Where is your beautiful modesty?
Go back, and do not return. The fear of
Allah is stronger in my heart than my
interest in you."

So, the maid went back to Sulaiman and told him what had happened. Sulaiman was very impressed by the piety of the *Mu'adhdhin*. Then Sulaiman summoned the *Mu'adhdhin*. When he entered Sulaiman's court, the guard told him:

"Congratulations! *Amir al-Mu'minin*
is pleased with you and has decided to give
you the maid in marriage and
with her, fifty thousand dirhams to
maintain her."

The *Mu'adhdhin* answered:

"Thank you for your generosity, but it is
not acceptable to me. By Allah, I
killed my desire for her from the first
time I saw her, and I dedicated it as a trust
for me with Allah (SWT). I would feel
ashamed to get back what I entrusted to
Allah (SWT)."

In spite of the *Mu'adhdhin's* refusal, Sulaiman

tried his best to persuade the *Mu'adhdhin* to accept the maid in marriage and receive the money. The *Mu'adhdhin* refused.

Sulaiman often wondered about him and would tell his friends about the piety of this man of God who expected the reward for his good deeds only from him.

Good Neighbor

Once 'Abd Allah Ibn al-Muqaffa' learned that
one of his neighbors was selling his house
to pay off his debts. Ibn al-Muqaffa' used to sit
in the shade of the house, so he said:

> Indeed, I do not fulfill my duty as a
> neighbor who has taken advantage of the
> shade of a neighbor's house, if he
> sells it in need of money, while I have it
> in excess."

Ibn al-Muqaffa' bought the house from him at
full price, and then offered it to his needy
neighbor as a gift.

Good Neighbors

Muhammad Ibn al-Jahm was in a financial
bind. He decided to put his house up for sale
for fifty thousand dirhams. A buyer liked
the house, but the high price surprised him. He
said to Ibn al-Jahm:

> "I am ready to buy the house, but the
> price you are asking is unusually high."

Ibn al-Jahm said to the buyer:

> "That is because my house is next to the
> home of Sa'id Ibn al-'As."

The buyer exclaimed:

> "Am I buying the house or the neighbor?"

Ibn al-Jahm replied:

> "Why not? A good neighbor must also
> be sold."

"What is so great in the neighbor of
Sa'id Ibn al-'As?" asked the buyer with
surprise.
Ibn al-Jahm replied calmly:
"There is value in being the neighbor of
one whom if you ask he gives, and if
you turn away from him he will turn to
you, if you do him disfavor he
does you a favor."

Sa'id Ibn al-'As heard this remark of Ibn
al-Jahm and was pleased. So he sent Ibn al-Jahm
one hundred thousand dirhams and told him:
"Keep your home, and don't leave
the neighborhood. A neighbor of a man
like Ibn al-Jahm has a value which
must not be lost."

Truthful Person

Rib'i from the tribe of Ashja' was known as a truthful person. His tribe claimed that he never lied in his life. A slanderer reported to al-Hajjaj Ibn Yusuf, the governor of Iraq, against Rib'i, saying:

> "There is a man from the tribe of Ashja', and his people claim that he has never lied, but indeed, he will lie to you today."

Al-Hajjaj asked:

> "How will he lie to me today?"

The man answered:

> "You drafted his two sons, but they disobeyed your orders, and stayed home."

The slanderer knew well that al-Hajjaj's
punishment for the disobedience to the order
of the draft would be death. Al-Hajjaj called
Rib'i over, and he came, an old man with
a crooked back.
Al-Hajjaj said to him:
　　"Are you Rib'i?"
He replied:
　　"Yes, I am Rib'i."
Al-Hajjaj asked:
　　"Where are your two sons?"
He replied unhesitatingly:
　　"They are both at home."
Al-Hajjaj was very much impressed by Rib'i's
truth and rewarded him with a horse
to ride and a garment. He also recommended
a special stipend be given him for the rest
of his life.

Remembering Allah

Mansur Ibn Mihran had a very pious slave girl.
Once, by mistake, she spilled a bowl full of
hot soup on him. His skin was burned and he
looked at her in anguish. She was
frightened but kept her cool and said:

"O teacher of good, remember Allah's
saying."

He asked:

"What is it?"

She replied:

"'And those who restrain their anger.'"

He said:

"I am restraining it."

She said:

> "And remember His saying, 'those who forgive people.'"

He said:

> "Alright, I forgive you."

She said:

> "And remember Allah (SWT) likes kind and beneficent people."

Mansur smiled and said:

> "Go. You are free."

Patience in Anger

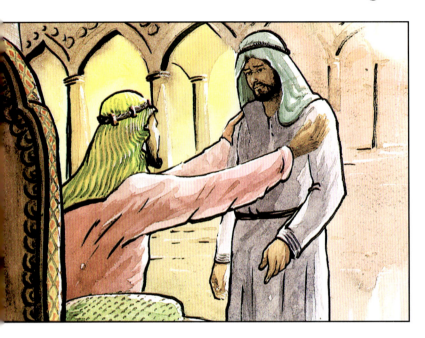

Once a man with whom 'Umar Ibn 'Abd
al-'Aziz was very angry came to him.
Instead of showing his anger, 'Umar said
to the man,

> "If I were not angry, I would have
> punished you."

It is reported, if 'Umar wanted to punish a
person he used to delay it for three days out of
fear of doing him injustice due to his anger.
And once 'Umar said to a man who

talked harshly to him,

Satan 1

"You intended to make Shaitan[1] provoke
me with the power of authority, so I'll
get from you here what you will get from
me on the Day of Judgment. Go
in peace. May Allah (SWT) bless you."

A Word of Honor

Al-Khalifah al-Walid Ibn Yazid wanted
to perform a pilgrimage to Makkah. A group of
leaders from Syria conspired to assassinate
him. They came to Khalid Ibn 'Abd Allah al-
Qasri and asked him to join them,
but he refused. Then they asked him to keep
their names a secret, and he agreed.
However, Khalid al-Qasri went to Khalid the
son of al-Walid Ibn Yazid and told him:

> "Tell *Amir al-Mu'minin*[1] not to go on the
> pilgrimage this year."

Khalid Ibn al-Walid asked:

> "But why should he not go on
> pilgrimage?"

Khalid al-Qasri said:

> "I sense some danger to his life."

Khalid Ibn al-Walid reported to his
father al-Qasri's advice. *Amir al-Mu'minin*
ordered al-Qasri to be brought to him.
When al-Qasri came, al-Walid asked him:

> "Is it true what my son said about
> your warning?"

He said:

> "Yes, *Amir al-Mu'minin*, so I fear."

Al-Walid asked al-Qasri to report to him
directly of what he had heard. Al-Qasri told the
story but withheld the names of the
conspirators. Al-Walid feared a big conspiracy

against him and asked:

"Who are those people? Tell me
their names."

Al-Qasri said:

"No, *Amir al-Mu'minin*, I have
promised the conspirators to keep their
names secret. I cannot break my
promise."

Al-Walid said:

"You must tell their names, or I will be
justified in thinking that you yourself are a
part of the conspiracy."

Khalid al-Qasri replied:

"I have given a word of honor I cannot
break it, O *Amir al-Mu'minin*."

Al-Walid said:

"Then I'll send you to Yusuf Ibn 'Umar
to punish you."

Khalid al-Qasri said:

"Even if you do that and I die, I will never
reveal their names to anyone."

So, al-Walid sent him to Yusuf instructing him
to use pressure techniques to find the
names of the conspirators. Yusuf was a harsh
and reckless person. He used everything
in his power to break al-Qasri's resolution but
al-Qasri remained firm. Finally, one day,
al-Qasri died of Yusuf's tortures, but even in
death, he remained true to his promise.

Who Should be Pitied

A man said to 'Amr Ibn 'Ubaid:
>   "I pity you for what people say about
>   you."
'Amr said:
>   "Do you hear me say anything about
>   them?"
The man said:
>   "No."
'Amr said:
>   "Then you should pity them."

Bribe

Caliph, 1
the head of Muslim
State.

Al-Khalifah[1] 'Abd al-Malik Ibn Marwan
summoned an official, who he learned had
accepted a gift. He asked him:
> "Did you accept a gift?"

The official answered:
> "O prince of the believers, your
> country is prosperous and your subjects
> are satisfied."

'Abd al-Malik said:
> "Answer what you are asked about."

The official then answered:
> "Yes, I accepted a gift."

'Abd al-Malik said:

> "If you accepted the gift, you naturally rewarded the giver by appointing him to a position which you never would have done if it were not for his gift. Indeed, you are dishonest. If you accepted it and did not reward him for it, indeed, you are wicked. And if you gave him similar to what you took, you are a low person. Any person who commits an act which indicates his wickedness, dishonesty and lowliness is not worthy of occupying a responsible position."

The Khalifah dismissed the official.

Making Shaitan[1] Unhappy

Once there was an ascetic who owned a sheep
which he liked very much. One day, he
came home to find that his sheep had lost a leg
and was standing on three legs only. He
asked his slave:

"Who did this to the sheep?"

The slave replied:

"I did it."

He asked:

"But why did you do it?"

The slave answered:

"Just to make you unhappy."

The ascetic said:

"Undoubtedly, I will make the Shaitan
unhappy, because he ordered you
to make me unhappy. Go! You are free."

Generosity

Al-'Abbas Ibn Muhammad was the financial
guardian of some needy person. One day,
he became angry with his beneficiary. The son
of al-'Abbas who handled the register of the
charity, left off the name of the man with whom
his father was angry.

When his father reviewed the list of the people
receiving charity, he discovered the
discrepancy. He asked:
    "Where is the name of that person?"

The son answered:

> "I knew you were angry with him, so I
> excluded his name from the recipients
> of charity."

Al-'Abbas advised:

> "Son, my anger does not preclude my
> gift. Indeed, your father never
> lets his anger affect his generosity."

Peace of Mind

Good fortune brought Talhah Ibn 'Ubaid Allah
unusual riches. It brought some relief but
also created many problems for him. He was
constantly pre-occupied with the idea of
what to do with the wealth. His wife Su'da Bint
'Awf one day noticed that he was depressed,
so she asked him:

    "What is the matter with you, Talhah?,
    I have never seen you so downhearted!"
Talhah replied:

    "The enormous amount of
    money I have gained has made me lose
    my peace of mind."

She retorted:

"You don't need to lose your peace of
mind. Call the people
and distribute it among them."

He liked the advice of his wife and said to his
servant:

"My boy! Call my people!. Let me
distribute it among them."

The servant made a public announcement and
people came in throngs and Talhah
continued to give. At the end of the day Su'da
asked the servant:

"How much money was given out?"

The servant replied:

"Four hundred thousand pieces."

Talhah had given away most of his money in
charity to attain the peace of mind. A wise man
heard this and remarked:

"If people know the pleasure of giving,
they would never bear the stain
of accumulating."

Wise Answer

A man came to 'Amir al-Sha'bi and started accusing him of various shameful acts. 'Amir remained unprovoked, then said to the man patiently:

> "May Allah (SWT) forgive you if what you said is untrue, and may Allah (SWT) forgive me if what you said is true."

Consultation

The famous 'Umayyad Khalifah 'Abd al-Malik
Ibn Marwan said:
>   "It is more preferable to err
>   with consultation than to do right
>   with despotism."

Biographical
Notes

Al-'Abbas Ibn Muhammad Abu al-Fadl al-Hashimi

121 H.-186 H. = 739 C.E.-802 C.E.

He was the brother of al-Mansur, who appointed him as
the governor of Syria. He became the governor of
al-Jazirah during the time of Harun al-Rashid. He died
in Baghdad. The quarter al-'Abbasiyah in Baghdad
was named after him.

'Abd Allah Ibn Ja'far

1 H.-80 H. = 622 C.E.-700 C.E.

'Abd Allah Ibn Ja'far Ibn Abu Talib Ibn 'Abd al-Muttalib
the Hashimite, the Qurashite. He was a Sahabi.
Born in Abyssinia, after his parents immigrated there,
he was the first Muslim to be born there. He
was nicknamed "The sea of generosity". He died
in al-Madinah.

'Abd Allah Ibn al-Muqaffa'

106 H.-142 H. = 724 C.E.-759 C.E.

He was a leading writer, the first in Islam to translate
books of logic. He originally a Persian, born in Iraq
as zoroastrian, and became a Muslim on the hands of
'Issa Ibn'Ali (al-Saffah's uncle). He translated
the book of (Kalilah and Dimnah) from Pahlavi into
Arabic. He wrote many books such as:
"al-Adabal-Saghir", "al-Adab al-Kabir" and "al-Yatimah."

'Abd al-Malik Ibn Marwan

'Abd al-Malik Ibn Marwan Ibn al-Hakam, the Umayyad,
the Qurashite, Abu al-Walid. One of the great
caliphs of Islam. Born and raised in al-Madinah, he was
a very learned man. Mu'awiyah appointed him as the
governor of al-Madinah when he was 26 years
of age. He became caliph after his father, Marwan, in
the year 65 H.,during his rule the government
records were transferred from Persian and Greek into
Arabic, and he was the first Muslim caliph to
mint dinars after 'Umar Ibn al-Khattab who minted the
dirhams. He died in Damascus.

'Amir al-Sha'bi

'Amir Ibn Sharahil al-Sha'bi al-Himyari, Abu 'Amr:
A *Tabi'i*, transmitter of hadith. He spent his entire life
in al-Kufah. He was a boon-companion of the
caliph 'Abd al-Malik. 'Umar Ibn 'Abd al-'Aziz appointed
him as a judge. He was *Faqih* and poet.

'Amr Ibn 'Ubaid

He was the Sheikh of the Mu'tazilites, and their *mufti*,
and one of the famous ascetics. He wrote many
treaties and books such as: "al-Tafsir" and "al-Radd
'ala al-Qadariyah." He died in Marra, near Makkah. The
caliph al-Mansur apologized to him, never had
such a thing happened before that a caliph apologized
to one of his subjects.

Al-Hajjaj Ibn Yusuf al-Thaqafi

He was an experienced leader, orator. Born and raised
in al-Ta'if (in al-Hijaz), he then moved to Syria,
where he joined Ruh Ibn Zinba' the police commander
for 'Abd al-Malik Ibn Marwan. He kept advancing
in his job as a soldier until 'Abd al-Malik appointed him
as a commander of the army which he dispatched
to fight 'Abd Allah Ibn al-Zubair in Makkah
and he defeated him, 'Abd al-Malik appointed him
governor of Iraq where he ruled for twenty years.
He constructed the city of Wasit (between al-Kufah and
al-Basrah, where he died.

Harun al-Rashid

He is the fifth Abbasid caliph and one of the most
famous among them. He became a caliph after
the death of his brother al-Hadi in the year 170 H. His
rule lasted for 23 years. He died in Sanabadh one
of the villages of Tus and was buried there. He was very
learned and highly educated. He used to go to
war against the Byzantines one year and went to Hajj
the next year.

Hatim al-Asam

Hatim Ibn 'Unwan, Abu 'Abd al-Rahman, known as
al-Asam (the deaf): Ascetic, very pious. He is originally
from Balkh, visited Baghdad and met with
Ahmad Ibn Hanbal. He participated in some liberation
campaigns (Futuh). Certain people nicknamed him
"Luqman of the Muslim Ummah." He died in Washjurd.

Rib'i Ibn Hirash

Rib'i Ibn Hirash Ibn Jahsh Ibn 'Amir the 'Absite,
Abu Maryam: A famous *Tabi'i* (second generation after
the Prophet) from the people of al-Kufah. He was
a trustworthy transmitter of hadith. It was reported that
he never told a lie. The story about him
proves that claim.

Qays Ibn Sa'd Ibn 'Ubadah

He was a Sahabi (companion of the Prophet) from the
tribe of Khazraj. He carried the banner of al-Ansar
with the Prophet (S). 'Ali appointed him as a governor
of Egypt. He died in al-Madinah al-Munawwarah.

Sa'id Ibn al-'As

Sa'id Ibn al-'As Ibn Sa'id Ibn al-'As Ibn 'Umayyah,
the Umayyad, Qurashite, Sahabi, one of the leading
Emirs participated in the Futuhat (liberation
campaigns). He liberated Tabaristan. 'Uthman Ibn
'Affan the third caliph appointed him a governor
of Kufah while he was young. Also
Mu'awiyah appointed him a governor of al-Madinah
and he stayed in that post until his death. He was
one of the committee who wrote the Qur'an for the
Caliph 'Uthman.

Sulaiman Ibn 'Abd al-Malik

Sulaiman Ibn 'Abd al-Malik, Abu Ayoub, was one of the
best of the Umayyad caliphs. Was born in the year
60 H., and died in the year 99 H. He was a just ruler.
He appointed 'Umar Ibn 'Abd al-'Aziz as a
caliph after him.

Talhah Ibn 'Ubaid Allah (Talhat al-Jud)

Talhah Ibn 'Ubaid Allah Ibn 'Uthman, the Taimi, the
Qurashite, Abu Muhammad, A Sahabi, one of
the most generous. He is one of the ten whom the
Prophet (S) promised Paradise, one of the six
people of the Shura, and one of the first eight muslims.

'Umar Ibn 'Abd al-'Aziz

61 H.-101 H. = 681 C.E.-720 C.E.

'Umar Ibn 'Abd al-'Aziz Ibn Marwan Ibn al-Hakam
the Umayyad, the Qurashite, Abu Hafs: The righteous
caliph, and the just ruler, very often, he is called
as the fifth rightly guided caliph. He was born
and raised in al-Madinah, and he became the governor
of al-Madinah for al-Walid Ibn 'Abd al-Malik. He
became caliph after Sulaiman Ibn 'Abd al-Malik. His
caliphate lasted two and half years only.

al-Walid Ibn Yazid

88 H.-126 H. = 707 C.E.-744 C.E.

Al-Walid Ibn Yazid Ibn 'Abd al-Malik Ibn Marwan,
Abu al-'Abbas: He became a caliph after his
uncle Hisham Ibn 'Abd al-Malik's death in the year
125 H., but he ruled only one year and
three months. He was a poet and a musician.

Yusuf Ibn 'Umar al-Thaqafi

d. 127 H. = 745 C.E.

Yusuf Ibn 'Umar Ibn Muhammad Ibn al-Hakam
al-Thaqafi: He was an Emir, a ruthless ruler during the
Umayyad period. He ruled Yaman for Hisham
Ibn 'Abd al-Malik, then Hisham transferred him to the
province of Iraq and added to it the province of
Khurasan. He survived until the time of Yazid Ibn
al-Walid, who dismissed him at the end of the
year 126 H., arrested him and jailed him in Damascus,
where he died at the age of sixty. He was
very generous

49

About the Translator

Dr. Assad Nimmer Busool

Dr. Busool was born in Rein-Nazareth, Palestine and received his bachelor and masters degrees in Arabic Literature and Islamic Studies from Hebrew University, Jerusalem. He received his masters degree in Library Science, and a Ph.D. in Arabic and Islamic Studies at the University of California at Berkley. He taught Arabic and Islamic Studies at San Diego State University and University of Minnesota, Minneapolis. Currently he is a professor and head of the department of Arabic Studies at American Islamic College, Chicago. Dr. Busool is a prolific writer and has published books and articles in English, Arabic and Hebrew.

Table of Contents